Acting Edition

SNOW DAY

BY TRACY WELLS

Copyright © 2026 by Tracy Wells
All Rights Reserved

SNOW DAY is fully protected under the copyright laws of the United States of America, the British Commonwealth, including Canada, and all member countries of the Berne Convention for the Protection of Literary and Artistic Works, the Universal Copyright Convention, and/or the World Trade Organization conforming to the Agreement on Trade Related Aspects of Intellectual Property Rights. All rights, including professional and amateur stage productions, recitation, lecturing, public reading, motion picture, radio broadcasting, television, online/digital production, and the rights of translation into foreign languages are strictly reserved.

ISBN 978-1-680-69090-3

www.playscripts.com
www.concordtheatricals.com

FOR PRODUCTION INQUIRIES
UNITED STATES AND CANADA
info@concordtheatricals.com
1-866-979-0447
UNITED KINGDOM AND EUROPE
licensing@concordtheatricals.co.uk
020-7054-7298

Each title is subject to availability from Concord Theatricals Corp., depending upon country of performance. Please be aware that *SNOW DAY* may not be licensed by Concord Theatricals Corp. in your territory. Professional and amateur producers should contact the nearest Concord Theatricals Corp. office or licensing partner to verify availability.

CAUTION: Professional and amateur producers are hereby warned that *SNOW DAY* is subject to a licensing fee. The purchase, renting, lending or use of this book does not constitute a license to perform this title(s), which license must be obtained from Concord Theatricals Corp. prior to any performance. Performance of this title(s) without a license is a violation of federal law and may subject the producer and/or presenter of such performances to civil penalties. Both amateurs and professionals considering a production are strongly advised to apply to the appropriate agent before starting rehearsals, advertising, or booking a theatre. A licensing fee must be paid whether the title(s) is presented for charity or gain and whether or not admission is charged. Professional/Stock licensing fees are quoted upon application to Concord Theatricals Corp.

This work is published by Playscripts, an imprint of Concord Theatricals Corp.

No one shall make any changes in this title(s) for the purpose of production. No part of this book may be reproduced, stored in a retrieval system, scanned, uploaded, or transmitted in any form, by any means, now known or yet to be invented, including mechanical, electronic, digital, photocopying, recording, videotaping, or otherwise, without the prior written permission of the publisher. No one shall share this title(s), or any part of this title(s), through any social media or file hosting websites.

For all inquiries regarding motion picture, television, online/digital and other media rights, please contact Concord Theatricals Corp.

MUSIC AND THIRD-PARTY MATERIALS USE NOTE

Licensees are solely responsible for obtaining formal written permission from copyright owners to use copyrighted music and/or other copyrighted third-party materials (e.g. artworks, logos) in the performance of this play and are strongly cautioned to do so. If no such permission is obtained by the licensee, then the licensee must use only original music and materials that the licensee owns and controls. Licensees are solely responsible and liable for clearances of all third-party copyrighted materials, including without limitation music, and shall indemnify the copyright owners of the play(s) and their licensing agent, Concord Theatricals Corp., against any costs, expenses, losses and liabilities arising from the use of such copyrighted third-party materials by licensees. For music, please contact the appropriate music licensing authority in your territory for the rights to any incidental music.

IMPORTANT BILLING AND CREDIT REQUIREMENTS

If you have obtained performance rights to this title, please refer to your licensing agreement for important billing and credit requirements.

CHARACTERS

MR./MRS. THOMPSON – School principal

PEGGY/PETE – Assistant to the principal

CHARLIE – Mail carrier

KID – Mysterious teen who is bundled up

TEEN – Inquisitive teen

PERSONS 1, 2 & 3 – People walking by

ELLIS – Worried sledder

BILLIE/BILLY – Excited sledder

ALEXIS – Dance committee chairperson

DYLAN – Dance committee member who has a secret crush

LOREN – Snow shoveler

JAMES – Loren's competition

VIV – A teen left out in the cold

BLAKE – A concerned neighbor

JETT – Snowball enthusiast

SAM – Jett's friend

MR./MRS. ANDREWS – Jett and Sam's teacher

SISTER/BROTHER – Jett and Sam's unsuspecting victim

VEX STORMWELL – An elf paladin LARPer

THISTLE SOGGYBOTTOM – A halfling bard LARPer

CODY – Four-time snowman-making champion

QUINN – A first-time snowman builder

KIT – A student ice skating instructor

MR./MRS. FRANKLIN – Kit's teacher

SETTING

Outside on a snowy day

TIME

Modern day

PRODUCTION NOTES

RUNTIME

Approximately thirty to forty-five minutes. You may cut scenes to create a shorter runtime. For a show around thirty minutes, choose eight of the scenes. For a forty-five minute show, stage all scenes.

CASTING

All roles allow for gender-flexible casting, and alternate names are provided for several characters. Please change references to names or pronouns for characters as needed.

COSTUMES

Students should be dressed in modern clothing with various items of outdoor winter attire such as hats, scarves, mittens, etc.

TIME-SPECIFIC REFERENCES

Feel free to change all mentions of social media, technology, etc. to anything that is timely and makes sense for your production.

ALTERNATE SCENE 4

An alternate, non-romance-related version of the "Snow Queen" scene is included at the end of the script. In the alternate version, the cast of the scene is as follows:

ALEXIS – Dance committee chairperson

NADIA, MADDIE, JEN & EMMA – Dance committee members and friends

SCENE BREAKDOWN

Scene 1: Snowed Under
Scene 2: Bundled Up
Scene 3: Out Cold
Scene 4: Snow Queen
Scene 5: Chill Out
Scene 6: Blanket of Snow
Scene 7: Tip of the Iceberg
Scene 8: The Snowball Effect
Scene 9: Winter Is Coming
Scene 10: A Frosty Reception
Scene 11: On Thin Ice
Scene 12: Cold Hands, Warm Heart
Scene 13: Snowed In

Scene 1: Snowed Under

(Outside of the school. **MRS. THOMPSON** *stands facing* **PEGGY**, *who is filming her on her phone.* **MRS. THOMPSON** *is wearing oversized sunglasses and a rain poncho, underneath which is a winter jacket and scarf.* **PEGGY** *has a bucket of "snow" next to her.)*

MRS. THOMPSON. Alright, let's try this again.

PEGGY. Snow day announcement video, take five!

(She points at **MRS. THOMPSON** *to go.)*

MRS. THOMPSON. *(In exaggerated, joyful tone.)* Hello Jefferson High[*] students and families! It's your principal, Mrs. Thompson, here with a very special announcement regarding school today. The sun may be shining –

(She takes off her glasses.)

And precipitation is falling –

(She holds her hand palm up and looks upward.)

But you won't find any rain outside.

(She starts to take off her poncho.)

Instead you'll find –

(She stops as she waits.)

I said, instead you'll find –

[*] Or Middle School

(She waits again, annoyed.)

MRS. THOMPSON. Peggy, that was your cue!

PEGGY. Oh, sorry!

(**PEGGY** *throws a handful of snow at* **MRS. THOMPSON**.)

MRS. THOMPSON. *(Annoyed.)* It's a little late now, Peggy. We'll have to start over.

PEGGY. It won't happen again, I promise. I was just so into your performance, Mrs. Thompson.

MRS. THOMPSON. We need to get through this so I can post the video and get back to work. The teachers and students may have a day off today, but snow days are my favorite days to get caught up.

PEGGY. *(Sarcastic.)* Yeah. Who wants to be at home, snuggled up in their nice, warm bed when you can be at work?

MRS. THOMPSON. Are you ready to do this, Peggy? Or would you rather crack jokes?

PEGGY. I'm ready. Let's take it from the top!

(**MRS. THOMPSON** *puts on her sunglasses and faces the camera.)*

Snow day announcement video, take six!

(She points at **MRS. THOMPSON** *to go.)*

MRS. THOMPSON. *(In exaggerated, joyful tone.)* Hello Jefferson High students and families! It's your principal, Mrs. Peggy –

(She stops.)

Now I'm all mixed-up. I said your name instead of mine.

PEGGY. It's okay. Just shake it off and start again.

(**MRS. THOMPSON** *shakes it off.*)

Snow day announcement video, take seven!

(*She points at* **MRS. THOMPSON** *to go.*)

MRS. THOMPSON. *(In exaggerated, joyful tone.)* Hello Thompson High – *(Annoyed.)* Now I'm mixing up the name of the school!

PEGGY. Just take a deep breath.

MRS. THOMPSON. I don't understand why we have to go through all this for a snow day! Can't we just send out an email or text blast and be done with it?

PEGGY. You know all the cool principals make video announcements like this and put them on Instabook and Tick Tack.

MRS. THOMPSON. You mean Instagram and TikTok.

PEGGY. That's what I said!

MRS. THOMPSON. Maybe I don't need to be a cool principal. Maybe I was happy being boring old Mrs. Peggy.

PEGGY. You mean boring old Mrs. Thompson.

MRS. THOMPSON. Right! Argh! Can we just get this done and over with before I forget my name entirely?

PEGGY. Of course we can. Snow day announcement video, take eight!

(*She points at* **MRS. THOMPSON** *to go.*)

MRS. THOMPSON. *(In exaggerated, joyful tone.)* Hello Jefferson High students and families! It's your principal, Mrs. Thompson, here with a very special announcement regarding school today. The sun may be shining –

(*She takes off her glasses.*)

And precipitation is falling –

(She holds her hand palm up and looks upward.)

MRS. THOMPSON. But you won't find any rain outside.

(She starts to take off her poncho.)

Instead you'll find –

*(**PEGGY** tosses snow at **MRS. THOMPSON**, who gets stuck in her poncho.)*

You've got to be kidding me!

*(**CHARLIE** enters wearing a mailbag and holding a stack of mail.)*

CHARLIE. Looks like you need a little help there, Mrs. Thompson.

MRS. THOMPSON. You think?

*(**CHARLIE** hands **PEGGY** the stack of mail and helps **MRS. THOMPSON** out of the poncho.)*

CHARLIE. There you go.

MRS. THOMPSON. Thanks, Charlie.

CHARLIE. What are you two doing out here?

PEGGY. We're filming a snow day video!

CHARLIE. The kids have a snow day today, huh? I bet they'll be excited.

MRS. THOMPSON. We're all excited. Trust me.

CHARLIE. But you're both here at the school.

MRS. THOMPSON. Snow days are the best days to get caught up with our work. Isn't that right, Peggy?

PEGGY. *(Wryly.)* Oh, yes. There's nowhere else I'd rather be.

MRS. THOMPSON. You still have to deliver mail even with all this snow, Charlie?

CHARLIE. Oh yes. *(Raising his hand and reciting.)* Neither snow nor rain nor heat nor gloom of night stays these couriers from the swift completion of their appointed rounds.

PEGGY. That's beautiful!

CHARLIE. That's the mail carrier's motto.

(He takes a bundle of mail out of his bag.)

And if I'm going to complete my rounds, I'd better get going. Have a great day!

MRS. THOMPSON. You too, Charlie.

*(She turns to **PEGGY**.)*

Now, let's get this video done so we can get back to work.

PEGGY. Snow day announcement video, take nine!

*(She points at **MRS. THOMPSON** to go.)*

MRS. THOMPSON. *(In exaggerated, joyful tone.)* Hello Jefferson High students and families! It's your principal, Mrs. Thompson, here with a very special announcement regarding school today. The sun may be shining –

(She takes off her glasses.)

And precipitation is falling –

(She holds her hand palm up and looks upward.)

But you won't find any rain outside.

(She starts to take off her poncho.)

Instead you'll find –

*(She takes off her poncho; **PEGGY** picks up the bucket of snow and dumps it on **MRS. THOMPSON**'s head. **MRS. THOMPSON** is not pleased.)*

MRS. THOMPSON. Snow.

 (**PEGGY** *stands next to* **MRS. THOMPSON** *and turns the camera to face her.*)

PEGGY. It's a snow day, everyone! Enjoy your day off from school!

 (**PEGGY** *waves at the camera as lights fade to black.*)

Scene 2: Bundled Up

*(Outside. **KID** is standing center, covered up in so many layers of winter gear that all we can see are his eyes. He stands still, unable to move, facing the audience until **TEEN** enters, carrying a tall thermos. **TEEN** starts to walk by and then stops and turns to **KID**.)*

TEEN. Hi.

(No response.)

Hello?

*(No response; **TEEN** starts waving a hand in front of **KID**'s face.)*

Hey, kid, that's an awful lot of winter gear you've got on. Are you alright in there?

(No response.)

Do you need some help? Are you stuck or something?

(No response.)

Are you alive in there?

*(Still no response. **PERSON 1** enters wearing a coat but no gloves and blowing into their hands, trying to keep them warm.)*

PERSON 1. It sure is cold out here. I wish I hadn't forgotten my gloves.

*(**KID** holds out his arm.)*

TEEN. He is alive!

PERSON 1. Were you worried he wasn't?

TEEN. I don't know. He was just standing there, covered in an enormous amount of clothing, not moving.

PERSON 1. Well, at least he's warm. I wish I had those gloves right about now.

(**KID** *shakes his arm up and down.*)

TEEN. I think he wants you to take his gloves.

(**KID** *nods.* **PERSON 1** *takes gloves. There are another pair of mittens underneath them.*)

PERSON 1. Thanks, kid!

(**PERSON 1** *puts on gloves and exits.*)

TEEN. That was nice of you.

(**PERSON 2** *enters from the opposite direction, not wearing a hat. She is bent forward, hurrying, trying to pull her coat up over her head. She bumps into* **TEEN.**)

PERSON 2. Sorry about that. I couldn't find my hat this morning, and it's freezing out here.

(**KID** *leans forward and wiggles his head.*)

TEEN. I think he wants you to take his hat.

PERSON 2. Are you sure?

TEEN. Pretty sure. He wiggled his arm just before giving someone a pair of gloves just a few minutes ago and now he's wiggling his head, which must mean he wants you to take his hat.

(**KID** *nods.*)

PERSON 2. Alright.

(**PERSON 2** *takes the hat and puts it on.* **KID** *has another hat on underneath.*)

Thank you. That's much better.

(**PERSON 2** *waves and starts to exit.*)

Have a good day!

(**PERSON 2** *exits.* **TEEN** *turns to* **KID**.)

TEEN. So is this how you plan to spend your snow day? Standing out here giving away hats and gloves?

(**KID** *shrugs or attempts to.*)

Well, this I've got to see!

(**TEEN** *stands to the side, watching* **KID** *as lights fade to black.*)

Scene 3: Out Cold

(The top of a snow hill. **ELLIS** *stands, holding a sled, looking down.)*

ELLIS. This is a terrible idea.

*(***BILLIE*** *enters excitedly, holding a sled. She stands a few feet away from* **ELLIS**, *looking forward.)*

BILLIE. This is a *great* idea!

ELLIS. Who wants to go sledding on our snow day instead of relaxing in front of the TV with a big bowl of popcorn?

BILLIE. Sledding is a much better way to spend a snow day than sitting around in front of the TV eating junk food.

ELLIS. There's no way I'm going to do this.

BILLIE. Let's do this!

*(***BILLIE*** *sees* **ELLIS** *and crosses over with her sled on her shoulder.)*

Oh, hey, Ellis!

ELLIS. Hey, Billie.

BILLIE. Isn't this the perfect day to go sledding?

ELLIS. If by perfect day, you mean there's snow on a hill, then I guess so.

BILLIE. *(Chuckling.)* Yeah, sledding would be a lot less fun without the snow, huh?

ELLIS. I'm guessing it would be pretty bumpy.

BILLIE. *(Chuckling.)* Bumpy, yeah, for sure!

*(***BILLIE*** *looks down, then, after a beat, looks at* **ELLIS**.*)*

So whenever you're ready.

ELLIS. Ready for what?

BILLIE. To go down the hill.

(**BILLIE** *points downward.*)

It's your turn. You were here first.

ELLIS. Oh...right.

(**ELLIS** *doesn't go.*)

BILLIE. Go ahead.

ELLIS. I don't know.

BILLIE. You don't know?

ELLIS. Yeah, I don't know if this was such a good idea. You go ahead.

(**ELLIS** *steps aside.*)

BILLIE. *(Incredulous.)* Wait a minute...are you scared to go sledding?

ELLIS. I mean...kind of.

BILLIE. Have you ever gone sledding before?

ELLIS. No. But my brother called me a chicken and told me not to come back home until I'd made it down to the bottom of this hill.

(**ELLIS** *points down.*)

This incredibly gigantic hill.

BILLIE. It's not that big.

ELLIS. Well, for me it is. You go on ahead. I'll just...be over here.

BILLIE. It's not scary, I promise. It's really a lot of fun. *(Smiling.)* There's nothing quite like the feeling of sitting on your sled, looking down the hill.

ELLIS. Oh, yes there is. It's called persistent nausea and bone-crushing fear.

BILLIE. And once the ride begins and you're sledding down the hill, you feel like a bird in flight!

ELLIS. Or maybe you feel like you should've made better life choices than throwing yourself down a slippery hill on ten cents worth of molded plastic.

BILLIE. I'm telling you, Ellis, you're going to love it.

ELLIS. I'm going to hate it.

BILLIE. The wind whipping through your hair as you soar down the hill...

ELLIS. The snow burning your cheeks as you careen headfirst into the ground...

BILLIE. The zigging, the zagging...

ELLIS. The screaming, the puking...

BILLIE. All of life's possibilities laid out before you...

ELLIS. My entire life flashing before my eyes...

BILLIE. I'm telling you...

BILLIE. You should do it!   **ELLIS.** I'm not gonna do it!

BILLIE. Really? I'm telling you, you're missing out.

ELLIS. And I'm telling you, I'd rather be knocked out cold by a sled than go riding down the hill on it.

(**CHARLIE** *enters carrying a mailbag and holding a stack of mail.*)

CHARLIE. Hey guys! What a great day for sledding!

(**BILLIE** *turns quickly toward* **CHARLIE.**)

BILLIE. Oh, hey, Charlie!

(*As* **BILLIE** *turns, her sled hits* **ELLIS**, *knocking her to the ground, out cold.*)

CHARLIE. Ellis!

> (**CHARLIE** *and* **BILLIE** *rush to* **ELLIS***'s side.*)

BILLIE. Ellis! Are you okay?

CHARLIE. I'll call the paramedics.

> (**CHARLIE** *takes out his phone and calls 911, stepping to the side as* **ELLIS** *wakes up and looks around.*)

ELLIS. Where am I?

BILLIE. You're at the top of the sledding hill.

ELLIS. *(Disappointed.)* Still?

CHARLIE. But don't worry, the paramedics are on their way and they'll get you to the bottom in no time.

ELLIS. I guess I can still tell my brother I made it down the hill after all!

> (**ELLIS** *thinks.*)

Quick question, though...how are they going to get me to the bottom?

CHARLIE. It's pretty cool, actually. You see, they have this sled –

ELLIS. No!

> (**CHARLIE** *and* **BILLIE** *look at each other as lights fade to black.*)

Scene 4: Snow Queen

(*Outside.* **ALEXIS** *enters, deflated, carrying a garland of cut-paper snowflakes. She wears a fancy dress with a scarf and earmuffs.* **DYLAN** *enters carrying a bag, which he drops as he rushes to* **ALEXIS**.)

DYLAN. I came as soon as I heard!

ALEXIS. I can't believe it.

DYLAN. I know.

ALEXIS. What are the odds?

DYLAN. A million to one, I'd guess.

ALEXIS. The weatherman said it was supposed to be clear skies all week!

DYLAN. Well, you never can trust a weatherman.

ALEXIS. But a snowstorm on the day of the Snowcoming Dance? (*Dramatically.*) It's too much to bear!

(**ALEXIS** *collapses in sobs.* **DYLAN** *bends down to console her.*)

DYLAN. Everything is going to be alright, Alexis. It's just a dance.

(**ALEXIS** *looks up, teary-eyed.*)

ALEXIS. Just a dance?

(*She stands, aghast.*)

JUST A DANCE?

(*She turns away from* **DYLAN**.)

How can you say such a thing when you know how hard I've been working on this?

DYLAN. I know. You're right. I'm sorry. I shouldn't have said that.

(**ALEXIS** *holds up the snowflake garland.*)

ALEXIS. Look at these snowflakes, Dylan.

(*She pushes them closer to his face.*)

LOOK AT THEM!

DYLAN. I'm looking, I'm looking!

ALEXIS. Do you know how long it took me to cut these out? How many hours of painstaking work went into each and every snowflake to make them as distinct and unique as the members of our entire student body?

DYLAN. I don't know...a lot?

ALEXIS. Yes, Dylan...a lot. Like, a lot, a lot. And do you know how many snowman sugar cookies I have sitting at home, each decorated with a sugar carrot nose and hat?

DYLAN. A dozen?

ALEXIS. Try twelve dozen.

DYLAN. (*Smirking.*) So that's like...a dozen dozen?

ALEXIS. (*Annoyed.*) Really, Dylan?

DYLAN. Sorry. I was just trying to lighten the mood. My bad.

ALEXIS. And do you know how much time I spent handpicking each song on the Snowcoming playlist?

DYLAN. Actually, I do know that one, because I was right there with you when we picked the songs.

ALEXIS. Oh, that's right. That was a fun night.

DYLAN. It sure was.

(**ALEXIS** *lifts the hem of her dress.*)

ALEXIS. But do you know how long it took me to find this dress? A dress so flowy, so sparkly, so perfect that only a queen should wear it.

DYLAN. *(Gently.)* A Snow Queen, maybe?

ALEXIS. *(Sadly, not thinking.)* Yes. *(Quickly.)* I mean no! I mean…of course I didn't expect to be crowned Snow Queen…but you never know…and if I was, I just wanted to look the part…and… *(Sighs.)* And now it's all for nothing. School's closed for a snow day and the dance is cancelled.

DYLAN. They could reschedule it, you know.

ALEXIS. No, they can't. I already talked to Mrs. Thompson. Apparently the cafetorium is booked solid for the next month. Peggy checked the calendar three times.

DYLAN. So that's it then?

ALEXIS. Yep. That's it.

(She holds up one end of the garland and looks at it.)

I guess I might as well throw these away.

(She starts to drop the snowflake garland.)

DYLAN. Wait!

(He rushes over and grabs the garland before it falls.)

ALEXIS. It doesn't matter anymore, Dylan. Don't you see?

DYLAN. I do see. I've seen it all along.

(He takes a step forward.)

Have you?

ALEXIS. What –

DYLAN. I've seen how much you care, not only about this dance, but about everyone at this school…how you wanted everything to be just right...how you wanted everyone to feel special. You wanted everything to be perfect.

ALEXIS. I did.

DYLAN. But for me, the most perfect thing isn't a paper snowflake or a sugar-cookie snowman. It's not even this beautiful dress.

(He takes her hand.)

It's you, Alexis. You're the reason I joined the dance committee. You're the reason I stayed up late picking songs. You're the reason I rushed over here the second I heard that the dance was cancelled.

(He picks up the bag and takes out a tiara.)

You're my Snow Queen, Alexis. And you don't need a dance to earn this crown.

(He puts the tiara on her head.)

ALEXIS. I...I don't know what to say.

*(**DYLAN** holds out his hand.)*

DYLAN. Say you'll dance with me?

ALEXIS. In the snow? Are you crazy?

DYLAN. Oh. Sorry.

(He takes a step back.)

ALEXIS. Only because it's freezing out here!

(She takes his arm and smiles.)

Let's go inside where it's warmer. We can turn on the playlist and dig into those snowman cookies.

DYLAN. Sounds good to me!

(They smile and exit as lights fade to black.)

Scene 5: Chill Out

(The bottom of a snow-covered driveway. **LOREN** *enters carrying a snow shovel and counting a wad of cash.)*

LOREN. Thirty-six...thirty-seven...thirty-eight.

(He folds up the bills and puts them in his pocket.)

Thirty-eight bucks for shoveling a few driveways. Not bad. Not bad at all. One more driveway and I'll have enough for that new Supersonic Adventure video game I've had my eye on.

*(***JAMES*** *enters from the opposite side of the stage, carrying a snow shovel and counting a wad of cash.)*

JAMES. Thirty-six...thirty-seven...thirty-eight.

(He folds up the bills and puts them in his pocket.)

Not bad. Not bad at all.

(He sees **LOREN**.*)*

Oh hey, what's up?

LOREN. Not much. Just out here making a few bucks.

JAMES. Same.

LOREN. Gotta love a snow day, huh?

JAMES. Yeah. Everyone else is sitting at home in their pajamas, watching cartoons, not realizing that there's real money to be made out here in the streets.

LOREN. Or on the sidewalks!

JAMES. Right!

(*They both laugh.*)

So what's your route?

LOREN. (*Pointing in the direction he came from.*) I started over on Maple and have been making my way east on Elm. You?

JAMES. (*Pointing in the direction he came from.*) I started on Acorn and cut across Pine, headed west.

LOREN. That's a good route. Lots of driveways on that route.

JAMES. For sure. I'm guessing between the two of us we've taken care of all the driveways in this neighborhood.

LOREN. Probably.

JAMES. Sounds like it's been a very profitable day for both of us.

LOREN. For sure, which is great 'cause I've been saving up for this new game...

JAMES. Supersonic Adventure?

LOREN. Yes!

JAMES. Me too!

LOREN. It looks amazing.

JAMES. The reviews are really good.

LOREN. I know. I've been wanting to play it forever.

JAMES. Me too. And now all that stands between me and Supersonic Adventure is...

(*Both **LOREN** and **JAMES** turn to look at the "house" behind them, then turn back to one another, realizing...*)

JAMES & LOREN. One more driveway.

> (**LOREN** *takes a step forward and plants his shovel.*)

LOREN. It's mine!

> (**JAMES** *also takes a step forward and plants his shovel.*)

JAMES. No, it's mine!

> (*They continue to take steps forward with each line until they are nose to nose. It should be over the top and humorous.*)

LOREN. I'm a better snow shoveler than you.

JAMES. You are out of your mind. I'm the best snow shoveler in town!

LOREN. Have you seen my edges?

> (**LOREN** *brings his fingers to his mouth.*)

Chef's kiss.

JAMES. Yeah, well which one of us has his pockets stuffed with salt?

> (**JAMES** *pulls out a handful of salt and sprinkles it on* **LOREN.**)

That's what I thought!

LOREN. This driveway has my name written all over it.

JAMES. I don't think so.

LOREN. Do you want me to show you? 'Cause I can write it for you here in the snow while I'm shoveling this driveway.

JAMES. If you put so much as one corner of that shovel on this driveway, you're going to be sorry.

> (**CHARLIE** *enters wearing a mailbag and carrying a stack of mail.*)

LOREN. You mean like this?

(**LOREN** *touches a corner of the shovel to the ground.* **JAMES** *holds up his shovel.*)

JAMES. Oh, it's *snooow* on!

(**LOREN** *picks up his shovel.*)

LOREN. You *snow* it is!

(**CHARLIE** *rushes over.*)

CHARLIE. Whoa, whoa, whoa! Put the shovels down!

(**LOREN** *and* **JAMES** *lower their shovels.*)

Now who can tell me what this fight is all about?

LOREN & JAMES. Supersonic Adventure!

CHARLIE. Supersonic what now?

LOREN. It's a video game. He and I both want it, but we're both two dollars short. Whoever shovels this driveway gets the money and the game.

CHARLIE. So this is over a video game?

LOREN AND JAMES. Yes.

CHARLIE. Got it. And how much do you charge to shovel a driveway?

LOREN & JAMES. Five dollars.

CHARLIE. So presumably, if you were to work together to shovel the driveway, you'd be able to split the five dollars, giving each of you enough money to buy the game.

LOREN. I guess so.

CHARLIE. And...now, hear me out for a minute...if you wanted, you could even play this video game together, is that correct?

JAMES. *(To* **LOREN.***)* You know, the reviews do say the game is better on two-player mode.

LOREN. Yeah, I saw that too. Wanna tag team this driveway then go play the game together?

JAMES. Sounds good.

(*They start to shovel.*)

CHARLIE. See? You can work out any problem when you show one another kindness and respect.

(**CHARLIE** *starts to cross away, perhaps whistling happily.*)

LOREN. You know I'm going to crush you when we reach those PvP rounds.

JAMES. I don't think so! That high score has my name written all over it!

LOREN. Oh, it's *snooow* on!

JAMES. You *snow* it is!

(**CHARLIE** *sighs and shrugs.*)

CHARLIE. All's fair in snow and video games.

(**LOREN** *and* **JAMES** *start shoveling as* **CHARLIE** *exits and lights fade to black.*)

Scene 6: Blanket of Snow

*(Outside. **VIV** enters wearing pajamas and boots. She's enrobed in a huge quilt or comforter and carrying a lawn chair. She plops down the lawn chair and sits grumpily. Moments later, **BLAKE** enters. He stops and bends down to look at the human-shaped quilt/comforter.)*

BLAKE. Viv, is that you?

VIV. Yep.

BLAKE. Why are you out here?

VIV. No reason.

BLAKE. There's gotta be a reason.

VIV. Nope.

BLAKE. You're in your pajamas.

VIV. I have snow boots on too.

BLAKE. And you're wrapped up in a quilt.

VIV. Hello? It's cold outside.

BLAKE. Which is why none of this makes sense at all. Come on, Viv, you have to tell me what you're doing out here!

VIV. I already told you...no reason.

BLAKE. So for no reason at all, you decided to come sit outside, wearing snow boots and pajamas, with only a quilt for warmth after the biggest snowfall this year?

VIV. That's right.

BLAKE. You can't possibly expect me to believe that.

VIV. And yet that's all the explanation you're going to get.

BLAKE. So you're just going to sit out here, wrapped up in a blanket?

VIV. Looks like it.

BLAKE. For how long?

VIV. That remains to be seen.

BLAKE. Do you at least have a hat and gloves?

VIV. Does it look like I have a hat and gloves?

BLAKE. I'm guessing you have some inside the house.

VIV. And that's where you would be wrong.

BLAKE. You don't have a hat or gloves inside your own house?

VIV. I'm sure I do. But the thing is...this isn't my house.

BLAKE. *(Intrigued.)* Ooh, the plot thickens!

> (**BLAKE** *presses his palms together and starts to tap his fingers against each other, his hands held under his chin as he paces around, thinking.)*

VIV. This isn't some big mystery, you know.

BLAKE. Oh, but it is!

(In detective mode.) I find you sitting outside, wearing only a pair of pajamas and snow boots, covered in a blanket for warmth, but with no hat or gloves. And then I find out this isn't even your house. So I have to ask myself...why would Viv sit outside a house that isn't hers in freezing cold temperatures? Why wouldn't she be home or off having some fun on her snow day?

VIV. I can't leave.

BLAKE. *(Alarmed.)* Are you being held against your will?

> (**BLAKE** *extends his arms and feels through the air.)*

Is there some sort of invisible force field that is keeping you within the confines of this property?

VIV. What? No.

BLAKE. Are you a prisoner? Perhaps you have a tracking device strapped to your ankle?

(**BLAKE** *tries to see* **VIV**'s *ankle, but she pulls it back.*)

VIV. Would you quit looking at my ankles? I'm not a prisoner.

BLAKE. Then why can't you leave?

VIV. Because it's a snow day.

BLAKE. What does that have to do with it? If anything, a snow day should give you more freedom, not get you stuck at some random house.

VIV. It does when your mom volunteers you to babysit for the neighbor's kids who are home from school while their parents have to go to work. Lucky me.

BLAKE. Ah, I get it now. Carry on then.

(**BLAKE** *starts to walk away, then stops and turns back.*)

But if you're supposed to be babysitting, then why are you outside?

(**VIV** *points behind her or offstage, at the house.*)

VIV. Have you met those kids? They're monsters! They pelted me with Nerf guns and chased me out of the house, locking the door behind them. I'm lucky I escaped with this quilt!

BLAKE. That's rough.

VIV. Tell me about it.

BLAKE. So how long is this babysitting job?

VIV. Oh, only another seven hours and forty-five minutes.

BLAKE. I'll be back with a hat and gloves.

(**BLAKE** *exits.*)

VIV. And some hot cocoa!

> (**VIV** *sits grumpily as a foam dart is shot and hits her in the head.*)

I hate snow days.

> (*Lights fade to black.*)

Scene 7: Tip of the Iceberg

*(Outside. **KID** is standing center, as before, though with a few layers removed. **TEEN** stands nearby.)*

TEEN. So where'd you get all these clothes from?

*(**KID** shrugs.)*

Don't get me wrong. It's a very cool idea. I like what you have going on here – it's very Good Samaritan and all that. But I mean, that is a *lot* of clothes you've got on there. Aren't you hot?

*(**KID** shrugs.)*

You've got to be hot.

*(**KID** thinks, then nods.)*

There's gotta be a way I can help you out a little. Maybe we could take off a layer or two?

*(**KID** shakes his head no.)*

Don't worry, we could donate them to a shelter or something.

*(**KID** shakes his head no.)*

Alright, then. We'll just have to figure something else out.

*(He walks around **KID**.)*

Looks to me like you have multiple jackets, at least three hats, several pairs of gloves, and a scarf.

(He picks up the end of a scarf.)

TEEN. If you took off just this scarf, I bet you'd feel a little cooler. Then I could hold it for you and when we see someone who really needs it, I'll give it to them. How does that sound?

>(**KID** *thinks, then nods.*)

Great. Then let's do this.

>(**TEEN** *starts to unravel the scarf, walking around* **KID** *as he does so.*)

This is a nice scarf.

>(*Still unraveling.*)

A long scarf, but a nice one. Pretty colors.

>(*Still unraveling.*)

Did someone make this for you?

>(**KID** *shrugs.*)

Well, whoever made it, it must've taken them a long time.

>(**KID** *nods as* **TEEN** *continues to unravel and* **CHARLIE** *enters carrying a mailbag.*)

Like, a really long time…a really, really long time!

CHARLIE. What have we got here?

TEEN. The world's longest scarf.

>(*He hands* **CHARLIE** *a handful of scarf.*)

Here, Charlie. Hold this for me, will you?

CHARLIE. Sure.

>(*As* **TEEN** *continues to unravel the scarf during the next few lines, the scarf gets wrapped around* **CHARLIE.**)

Say, how much more scarf do you have there?

TEEN. I honestly don't know, but by the looks of things, this is just the tip of the iceberg.

(*He continues unraveling.*)

CHARLIE. Are you sure this is even a scarf? It's way too long!

(**KID** *nods.*)

Maybe this was meant to be a blanket and whoever made it didn't know how to add rows, so they just kept going in a straight line.

TEEN. Or maybe there's a giant somewhere with a super huge neck who's wondering where his scarf went.

(**KID** *shrugs.*)

CHARLIE. Either way, you've got to be getting to the end soon. I've got mail to deliver.

(*He looks down and sees he's wrapped up.*)

If I can get out of this scarf, that is.

TEEN. Oh, sorry about that, Charlie.

(*He unravels* **CHARLIE**, *perhaps spinning him out of the scarf.*)

There you go.

CHARLIE. Thanks. And good luck with that scarf.

TEEN. Thanks.

(**CHARLIE** *exits as* **TEEN** *pulls the last bit of scarf off of* **KID**.)

There you go! How do you feel?

(**KID** *nods.*)

TEEN. Good. Now there's just one thing left to do…

  *(**KID** holds up his arms questioningly.)*

We've got to find the giant who lost this scarf!

  *(**KID** and **TEEN** look around as lights fade to black.)*

Scene 8: The Snowball Effect

(Outside. A mound of snow big enough for **JETT** *and* **SAM** *to hide behind is on one side of the stage. A pile of snowballs is next to the snow mound.* **JETT** *is behind the snow mound, unseen.* **SAM** *enters carrying snowballs.* **JETT** *unexpectedly pops up from behind the snow mound, a snowball in his hand.)*

JETT. Think fast!

(He throws a snowball at **SAM**.*)*

SAM. *(Yells.)* Ah! Would you stop, Jett? Every time I come back from making snowballs, you throw one at me.

JETT. Then maybe you're the one that needs to stop…stop being so jumpy, that is!

*(***SAM*** puts his snowballs in the pile.)*

SAM. I think we've got enough now.

JETT. Yeah, that should be fine, for now, anyway.

SAM. How long are we going to be out here?

JETT. Long enough to smack my sister* square in the face with a snowball!

SAM. And you're sure she'll be coming this way?

JETT. Oh, definitely. My mom sent her to the store for some bread an hour ago, which means she took her sweet time walking around the store, looking at the shampoo and the beauty products and the candy. When she's finally done browsing, she'll get the bread and go to the checkout line. Then once she pays, she should be on her way.

SAM. Which will be…

* Or brother

JETT. Any minute, Sam! Any minute...

SAM. And how will we know it's her?

JETT. She's my sister! I'm stuck living with her every day. I'm pretty sure I'll know her when I see her.

SAM. I just meant, what color coat is she wearing? Does she have a hat on? There's a lot of people walking around today and playing in the snow. I just want to make sure we get the right person.

JETT. Fair enough. I'm pretty sure she has on a red* coat with a white* hat and gloves.

SAM. That works for me.

JETT. Oh, and of course she'll have a Dooley's Market shopping bag.

SAM. Right. Good thinking.

> (**SAM** *looks around.*)

Hey! I think that's her now!

> (**JETT** *and* **SAM** *duck behind the snow mound, peeking as* **MRS. ANDREWS** *enters, head down, carrying a Dooley's Market grocery bag. She stops just onstage, so that most snowballs will fly offstage.*)

JETT. That's her, alright! Let 'er rip!

> (**JETT** *and* **SAM** *throw snowballs rapid-fire at* **MRS. ANDREWS**.*)

MRS. ANDREWS. What's going on? What's happening?

SAM. *(As he throws a snowball.)* Take that!

> (**MRS. ANDREWS** *tries to deflect snowballs with her arm or bag.*)

---

*Feel free to change the colors to whatever you like or have on hand. Just make sure Mrs. Andrews and Sister wear the same color coat, hat, and gloves.

MRS. ANDREWS. Cut that out!

JETT. That's for the time you used up all the hot water! And that's for the time you told Mom and Dad about my D in math, and that's for the time you called me a platypus!

SAM. A platypus?

JETT. We don't talk about that.

> (**JETT** *throws another snowball.*)

And that's for not sharing the last piece of chocolate cake!

SAM. Yeah! That wasn't nice!

MRS. ANDREWS. *(Shielding her eyes.)* Sam? Jett? Is that you?

SAM. *(Realizing.)* Um....Jett?

JETT. Eat snow, you platypus!

MRS. ANDREWS. *(Angrily.)* Sam and Jett, you stop that this instant!

SAM. Jett, I don't think that's your sister.

JETT. Of course it's my sister! She's wearing a red coat and white hat and she's carrying a Dooley's Market bag.

> (**JETT** *throws a snowball.*)

Who's the platypus now, sis?

> (**MRS. ANDREWS** *starts marching toward* **SAM** *and* **JETT.***)

MRS. ANDREWS. You boys are going to be in big trouble!

SAM. No, seriously, Jett. That's not your sister. That's –

> (**MRS. ANDREWS** *is now right in front of their snow mound, angry, with her arms folded.*)

SAM & JETT. Mrs. Andrews!

JETT. Oh, um, hi Mrs. Andrews. I didn't see you there.

MRS. ANDREWS. It seems like you saw me just fine while you were hurling snowballs at my face!

SAM. We didn't know it was you, I swear. We thought you were his sister.

JETT. You know how it is, Mrs. Andrews… We don't expect to see teachers out in the wild.

MRS. ANDREWS. In the wild?

JETT. You know what I mean…in the real world.

SAM. Especially on a snow day.

JETT. We're really sorry, Mrs. Andrews. It won't happen again.

MRS. ANDREWS. It had better not.

      (**MRS. ANDREWS** *brushes off her coat.*)

Now, pack up those snowballs and hurry home before you cause any more damage. It may be a snow day today, but you still have a math test tomorrow.

SAM & JETT. Yes, Mrs. Andrews.

      (**MRS. ANDREWS** *exits.* **SAM** *and* **JETT** *watch her exit.*)

JETT. Phew! That was a close one.

SAM. No kidding.

      (**SISTER** *enters carrying a Dooley Market bag.*)

Hey, isn't that your sister?

JETT. Get her!

      (**SAM** *and* **JETT** *grab a bunch of snowballs and chase* **SISTER** *offstage, throwing snowballs at her as lights fade to black.*)

Scene 9: Winter Is Coming

(*Outside.* **VEX STORMWELL** *is center stage with a sword, going through elaborate sword-fighting choreography. He wears a full paladin costume, which can be handmade, but should be made fairly well. He has elf ears.*)

VEX. (*Dramatically.*) Vile creature! I'll send you back to where you came from!

(**VEX** *swings his sword and makes sword-swinging noises.*)

Come at me again, tyrant, and I'll chase you down to the depths of the abyss!

(**VEX** *swings his sword and makes sword-swinging noises.*)

Evil has no place here. Now feel the wrath of my vorpal sword!

(**VEX** *swings his sword and makes sword-swinging noises.* **THISTLE SOGGYBOTTOM** *enters carrying a small ukulele. Her costume is clearly homemade and not very well-made. She is looking at her phone.*)

(*Seeing* **THISTLE**.) Halt, stranger! You are unfamiliar in these parts and must identify yourself if you are to be given safe passage.

THISTLE. Oh, hey. Is this the Caverns and Creatures Role-playing Meetup?

VEX. Meetup? As in, a group of wandering swordsmen banding together to fight a common enemy? If so, then this is the place.

THISTLE. On the message board it just calls it a meetup.

*(She shows **VEX** her phone.)*

THISTLE. It's right here.

*(**VEX** takes a step back, affronted.)*

VEX. What is this magical totem you are presenting before me? Is this an agent of sorcery? Are you a cleric, stranger?

THISTLE. A cleric? Oh, no. I'm a halfling.

VEX. *(Aside, not in character.)* A halfling is actually your race. Like how I'm an elf.

(He points to his ears.)

What you're looking for is your class.

THISTLE. My class?

VEX. Kind of like your job? Like I'm a paladin, which is a kind of knight who fights for a cause.

THISTLE. That's cool!

VEX. So what is your class?

THISTLE. Oh, right… I'm a bard.

(She holds up her ukulele.)

See? I brought my lute.

VEX. *(Back in character.)* That doesn't look like any lute I've seen before in these parts.

THISTLE. Well, it's actually a ukulele. I don't actually have a lute, but I thought this would be fine.

VEX. *(Not in character again.)* It's fine. Don't worry about it.

THISTLE. Thanks.

VEX. So tell me, stranger, what is your name?

THISTLE. You're going to love this. I came up with it using one of those name generators they have online…

VEX. *(Sighs.)* Of course.

THISTLE. It's Thistle Soggybottom!

VEX. *(Not in character.)* Thistle Soggybottom? Really?

THISTLE. Isn't it hilarious? I just love it.

VEX. I'm sure you do.

THISTLE. And what's your character's name?

VEX. *(Back in character, dramatically raising his sword.)* My name, young halfling, is Vex Stormwell!

THISTLE. Wow! Cool!

VEX. Yes, it is quite cool in these northern lands on which the snow has softly fallen.

THISTLE. No, I just meant – *(Realizes.)* Oh, I get it.

(Holds out her ukulele.) Hazzah!

(Aside.) Did I do that right?

VEX. Do it right?

(Not in character.) Let me guess… This is your first time LARPing?

THISTLE. LARPing?

VEX. Live-Action Role-Playing?

THISTLE. Right. Yes it is.

VEX. *(Sarcastically.)* Great.

THISTLE. I just thought it sounded cool and we had a snow day today and I had nothing better to do, so I thought, why not!

VEX. Got it.

THISTLE. So where is everyone?

(She looks at her phone.)

The message board said this was a "once-in-a-season chance for an epic battle on a snow-covered landscape."

VEX. That's right. It is! I've been dying to do a role-playing campaign on a snowy day but the weather hasn't cooperated. I thought a lot of people would be into it, but...well, you're the only one who's shown up.

THISTLE. That stinks.

VEX. Yeah. It's kind of a bummer. We can't really have an epic battle with one elf paladin and one halfling bard.

THISTLE. Why not?

VEX. Well, for one thing, bards aren't known for being particularly good swordsmen.

THISTLE. Oh good, because I didn't bring a sword. Just my lute.

VEX. Your ukulele. And I have extra swords.

THISTLE. You do?

VEX. Yeah, but it doesn't really matter. We should probably just go home. Sorry your first LARP meetup was a flop.

THISTLE. But it's a once-in-a-season chance!

VEX. I know, but what can we do?

THISTLE. *(Getting into character.)* I have an idea, my liege.

    (She bows dramatically.)

VEX. *(Back in character.)* No need to bow. I'm not your king.

THISTLE. Right.

    (She straightens up.)

In service to the realm, I give up my lute and my title as bard.

VEX. *(Confused.)* Why would you do that, young halfling?

THISTLE. So that I might also become a paladin and fight for a cause.

VEX. And what is your cause, paladin?

THISTLE. To fight an epic battle on a snow-covered landscape.

> *(She bows and holds out her ukulele.* **VEX** *smiles and takes it.)*

VEX. Very well.

> *(He exchanges her ukulele for a sword, which he uses to knight her.)*

I now pronounce you Thistle Soggybottom...

(Out of character.) Are you sure about that name?

THISTLE. Yes. Yes I am.

VEX. Alright.

> *(He resumes knighting her.)*

I now pronounce you Thistle Soggybottom, a halfling paladin. Now rise and accept your blade.

> *(He hands her the sword.)*

THISTLE. Ooh! My very own sword.

VEX. What are you going to name it?

THISTLE. I get to name it?

VEX. Of course.

THISTLE. Let's see what the online name generator suggests!

> *(She takes out her phone.)*

How about Sticky Tooth? Or maybe Fluffy Bunny?

VEX. You've got to be kidding me.

THISTLE. Ooh! Knitting Needle!

> *(**THISTLE** swings her sword around as **VEX** shakes his head and lights fade to black.)*

Scene 10: A Frosty Reception

*(Outside. An elaborately carved or decorated snowman is center. **CODY** is tending to it, putting on the finishing touches. Next to it is a plain snowman made only of three progressively smaller balls stacked on top of one another with no decorations.)*

CODY. *(Placing glasses on the snowman's face.)* That should just about do it.

(He stands back to assess his work.)

Not bad, if I do say so myself. Not bad at all.

*(***QUINN*** enters with a paper grocery bag containing simple snowman decorations – a carrot nose, coal or dark stones, buttons, a scarf, a hat, a wooden pipe, and a couple of sticks.)*

QUINN. That looks great!

CODY. Thanks! It's my take on the classic Dickens tale *A Christmas Carol.*

QUINN. Oh, I see it...Ebenezer Scrooge, right?

CODY. Exactly! I got this scarf and hat from the local historical society.

QUINN. They're a really nice touch.

CODY. *(Pointing out features, but they need not be visible to the audience.)* And you can see here when I've carved in his adventures with the Ghost of Christmas Past. And over here, you can see his travels with the Ghost of Christmas Present.

QUINN. Cool!

CODY. Yeah, it took me about twelve hours or so, I would say.

QUINN. I'm guessing you've entered the snowman-building competition before.

CODY. You're looking at the four-time snowman-building champion right here.

QUINN. Impressive!

CODY. I think it comes down to a smart theme and expert execution.

QUINN. Well, if that's what you need, then I bet you've got your fifth championship win right there. (*Indicates snowman.*)

CODY. Here's hoping the judges agree.

QUINN. I'm sure they will.

CODY. (*Aside.*) You're not a judge, by any chance, are you?

QUINN. Me? A judge? (*Chuckles.*) I don't think so. I'm actually here to compete.

CODY. No kidding?

(**CODY** *looks around.*)

Which one of these snowmen is yours?

QUINN. This one right here. (*Indicates plain snowman.*)

CODY. This one? But it's not even decorated!

QUINN. Give me a minute and it will be.

(**QUINN** *puts down their bag and decorates their snowman, then steps aside.*)

Ta-da!

CODY. That's it?

QUINN. Yep. What do you think?

CODY. But it took you like...two minutes.

QUINN. I know! Isn't that great?

CODY. And you don't have any carvings or historically accurate costume accessories or anything!

QUINN. Yeah, I pretty much just grabbed this stuff from home.

CODY. So how can you possibly think you might win a snowman-making competition with a plain old boring snowman like that?

> *(As he says that, **CHARLIE** enters wearing his mailbag and carrying a clipboard, pen, one first place ribbon, and an honorable-mention ribbon. He crosses to **CODY** and **QUINN**.)*

CHARLIE. A snowman like this? Why, I'd say it's a classic!

> *(He makes check marks on his clipboard as he lists items.)*

Carrot nose...button smile...corncob pipe.

> *(He hands the honorable-mention ribbon to **QUINN**.)*

I'd say this is the best authentic Frosty I've seen today. Great job.

QUINN. *(Reading ribbon.)* Honorable Mention in the Classic Frosty Division. Nice!

CODY. You know...I guess there is something to be said for a classic after all.

CHARLIE. That's right. And there's also something to be said for hours of hard work and planning and craftsmanship.

> *(He hands **CODY** the first-place ribbon.)*

Nice job, Cody.

CODY. Thanks!

> *(**CODY** looks at the ribbon as **CHARLIE** exits.)*

QUINN. Congratulations!

CODY. Thanks! You too...really. I think sometimes I get so caught up in the details that I forget that simple is beautiful too.

QUINN. Do you want to go somewhere and celebrate our wins? There's a hot cocoa stand set up over there that has double-fudge hot chocolate with a peppermint swirl and a hand-spun marshmallow on top with peppermint shavings.

CODY. Sounds a little over the top to me.

(**CODY** *smiles.*)

I don't know about you, but right now, I'm in the mood for something simple...something classic.

QUINN. Two plain hot chocolates coming right up!

(**QUINN** *and* **CODY** *smile and exit as lights fade to black.*)

Scene 11: On Thin Ice

(Outside, near an ice rink. A bench is center on which is a small bell and a sign that reads "Ice Skating Lessons, Today Only, $20. Ring Bell for Service." **MRS. FRANKLIN** *enters carrying a pair of ice skates. The ice skates should have guards on them. Perhaps there is also some sort of mat underneath for when she stands on the skates. You could also use roller skates or Heelys.)*

MRS. FRANKLIN. Ice skating lessons.

(She holds up her ice skates.)

This must be the place.

(She rings the bell, then sits down. She bends down and starts unlacing her boots as **KIT** *enters, not recognizing* **MRS. FRANKLIN** *at first.)*

KIT. *(Energetically.)* Hello there, skater, and welcome to the most exciting day of your life...the day you learn to ice skate!

(During the next line, **MRS. FRANKLIN** *slowly looks up.)*

My name is Kit and I'm going to be your teacher to–

*(***KIT*** stops.)*

MRS. FRANKLIN. *(Narrowing her eyes.)* It's you.

KIT. *(Nervous.)* Mrs. Franklin...what are you doing here today?

MRS. FRANKLIN. Well I was going to have an ice skating lesson but I see now this was a bad idea.

(She reties her boots and stands, holding her ice skates.)

KIT. Mrs. Franklin, wait! You don't have to go.

MRS. FRANKLIN. It's okay, Kit. Really.

> *(She starts to exit.)*

KIT. But you wanted to learn how to ice skate!

MRS. FRANKLIN. I don't want to learn that bad.

KIT. I'm a really good teacher, I swear.

> *(**MRS. FRANKLIN** stops and turns back.)*

MRS. FRANKLIN. If you're as good at teaching ice skating as you are at goofing around in class, then I'm sure you're the greatest ice skating teacher in town. Unfortunately, I am just not in the mood to be teased tomorrow in front of my other students.

> *(She resumes exiting.)*

KIT. I wouldn't do that, I swear.

MRS. FRANKLIN. Sorry, Kit, but I don't believe you. Have a nice rest of your snow day.

> *(**MRS. FRANKLIN** is almost to the exit.)*

KIT. *(Calling out.)* But you're my only customer!

> *(**MRS. FRANKLIN** stops and sighs.)*

MRS. FRANKLIN. And?

KIT. And I could really use the money. My mom says I need to help save for college, and since it's a snow day, I thought this would be a good way to earn some extra cash.

MRS. FRANKLIN. Your college account? Are you sure this isn't one of your tricks to weasel into my soft, caring teacher heart so that I'll stay?

KIT. *(Hopefully.)* I don't know...is it working?

MRS. FRANKLIN. Fine.

(**MRS. FRANKLIN** *crosses back to bench.*)

MRS. FRANKLIN. But I swear if you breathe one word of this to anyone at school, I'm giving you detention for a week. Do you hear me?

KIT. Yes, Mrs. Franklin. Thank you, Mrs. Franklin!

MRS. FRANKLIN. So what's first?

KIT. Well, the first thing you have to do is put on your skates.

MRS. FRANKLIN. *(With a withering look.)* Yes, I'm aware.

(**MRS. FRANKLIN** *bends down and starts putting on skates during the next few lines.*)

KIT. Right. So before we begin, I should ask if you have any previous ice skating experience.

MRS. FRANKLIN. Other than when I was a kid and fell flat on my butt, no, I don't.

(**KIT** *is snickering but trying not to.*)

It's because I said "butt," right?

KIT. I mean, it's just too funny to hear a teacher saying the word "butt."

(**KIT** *laughs.*)

MRS. FRANKLIN. Right now I'm not your teacher...I'm your client, remember?

KIT. Of course. Sorry.

(**KIT** *controls her laughter, then resumes, seriously.*)

So no recent ice skating experience?

MRS. FRANKLIN. No.

KIT. And what made you decide to learn how to ice skate?

MRS. FRANKLIN. You won't tell everyone in class tomorrow and make fun of me?

KIT. I promise.

(**MRS. FRANKLIN** *looks around, then leans in.*)

MRS. FRANKLIN. It's the costumes.

KIT. The costumes?

MRS. FRANKLIN. You know? The ones figure skaters wear. The spandex and the Lycra, the glitter and the sequins?

KIT. Whoa. I did not see that coming!

MRS. FRANKLIN. *(Excited.)* And that's not all! Have you seen the touring kids shows? There's skating mice and lions and...princesses!

(She sighs.)

KIT. Mrs. Franklin, are you telling me you secretly want to be an ice skating princess?

MRS. FRANKLIN. *(Lost in her daydream.)* Would I ever!

(She snaps out of it.)

I mean, no! Of course not!

(She leans in.)

(Threateningly.) If you tell anyone, it's detention for two weeks!

KIT. I won't tell anyone, trust me.

MRS. FRANKLIN. You'd better not.

KIT. Besides, who would believe me? Mrs. Franklin in a bedazzled spandex princess costume!

(She laughs.)

MRS. FRANKLIN. Are you going to give me a lesson or not?

KIT. Oh, right.

> *(She holds out her hand and bows.)*

Your Highness.

> *(**MRS. FRANKLIN** gives **KIT** a look, but takes her hand and stands. At first, she's feeling okay, then suddenly, she starts to wobble. Then she falls down on her behind.)*

Or should I say, Your Lowness!

> *(**KIT** starts giggling. **MRS. FRANKLIN** is annoyed.)*

MRS. FRANKLIN. That's it! Detention for a month!

KIT. Totally worth it!

> *(**MRS. FRANKLIN** tries to get up. **KIT** reaches out and they both fall, then look at one another and laugh as lights fade to black.)*

Scene 12: Cold Hands, Warm Heart

(*Outside.* **KID** *is standing center, as before, down to just a coat or sweater, a ski mask, and a pair of gloves.* **TEEN** *stands nearby.*)

TEEN. Looks like you're almost done.

(**KID** *looks down, then shrugs.*)

You've only got a couple pieces of clothing left to give.

(**KID** *nods.*)

If you give them away, you're going to be pretty cold. It's been snowing all day.

(**KID** *nods.*)

Don't say I didn't warn you.

(**KID** *shrugs.*)

You know, we've been out here all day, you and I, and I don't even know who you are behind that ski mask. Are you a kid or a grown-up? Have we met before or are you a total stranger? And what is your reason for doing all this? You stand there and you say nothing.

(**KID** *shrugs.*)

Okay. If that's how you want it.

(**PERSON 3** *enters, obviously cold, wearing only a thin jacket that they have pulled tight around themselves.* **KID** *crosses to* **PERSON 3**. **KID** *takes off his gloves and holds them out.*)

PERSON 3. Oh, no. I couldn't possibly take your gloves.

(**KID** *holds them out insistently.*)

PERSON 3. Are you sure?

> (**KID** *nods.* **PERSON 3** *takes his gloves and puts them on.*)

Thank you. This helps a lot. It's freezing out here.

> (**KID** *points to his ski mask and starts to take it off.*)

TEEN. Is this it? Is this the moment their secret identity is finally revealed?

PERSON 3. *(Clasping **KID***'s *hands.)* No. That's okay. You keep it. The gloves are more than enough.

> (**PERSON 3** *smiles and exits.* **KID** *crosses back to* **TEEN**, *rubbing his hands together and blowing on them as* **CHARLIE** *enters, unseen by* **TEEN**, *carrying a mailbag and holding a stack of mail.*)

TEEN. So, that's it? You're not going to take off the mask? We're not going to know who you are?

CHARLIE. Oh, I think we all know who they are.

TEEN. We do?

CHARLIE. Of course. They are kind and generous. They put the needs of others before themselves. They act selflessly and considerately. They give what they have, even when they don't have much to give. And when things are tough, there they are, standing, right where you need them.

TEEN. *(Smiles.)* Yeah. I guess you're right. That's who they are.

CHARLIE. *(To **KID**.)* Looks like you're about done for the day. Are you getting ready to head home?

> (**KID** *nods.*)

Good.

> (**CHARLIE** *hands him a stack of mail.*)

Then here's your mail.

> (**KID** *accepts the mail and smiles.*)

See you tomorrow, kid.

> (**KID** *nods and* **CHARLIE** *exits.* **KID** *leafs through his mail, then tucks it away, blowing on his cold hands.*)

TEEN. Looks like your hands are pretty cold, huh?

> (**KID** *nods.* **TEEN** *holds up his thermos.*)

I have a thermos of hot cocoa here, if you want some. It's not much, but maybe, at least for now, it'll keep you warm.

> (**KID** *nods.* **TEEN** *opens a thermos and pours hot cocoa into the lid/cup and gives it to* **KID**. **KID** *and* **TEEN** *"cheers" with the lid/cup and thermos, then take a drink as lights fade to black.*)

Scene 13: Snowed In

(Outside of the school. **MRS. THOMPSON** *and* **PEGGY** *enter.* **MRS. THOMPSON** *has a snow shovel and* **PEGGY** *has a car scraper/brush.)*

MRS. THOMPSON. Well, Peggy, I think we can safely say we've put in a good day's work.

PEGGY. If you mean spending hours and hours within these walls filling out endless amounts of paperwork until our hands cramp and our fingers bleed, then yes, Mrs. Thompson...we sure did!

MRS. THOMPSON. Now all we have to do is shovel a path to our cars and we can go home.

(She looks around, confused.)

If we can even find our cars, that is.

PEGGY. It sure has snowed a lot more since we've been at work.

MRS. THOMPSON. You're not kidding!

(She shovels a little.)

I don't think this shovel is going to make a dent in all this snow.

PEGGY. Let me try.

("Brushes" at the snow – this can be mimed.)

MRS. THOMPSON. Is that a snow brush from your car?

PEGGY. Yes! Wasn't it quick thinking of me to bring it inside this morning?

MRS. THOMPSON. *(Sarcastically.)* Oh, yes. It's going to come in real handy right about now.

PEGGY. I can go inside and see if we have another shovel.

(She turns to exit.)

MRS. THOMPSON. Don't bother. If the parking lot is this bad, the roads are going to be worse. I hate to say it, Peggy, but I think we're stuck here for the night.

PEGGY. Snowed in? At the school?

MRS. THOMPSON. Looks like it.

(She turns to exit.)

Let's see if they have anything good to make for dinner in the cafeteria kitchen.

PEGGY. Ooh! Maybe they have leftover meatloaf!

MRS. THOMPSON. And maybe we can stack up some gym mats and make beds.

PEGGY. Yes! And we can use one of the teacher's projectors to watch a movie!

MRS. THOMPSON. I probably have a copy of the drama club's production from last year.

PEGGY. *Guys and Dolls*? That one was really good. Let's do it!

*(**PEGGY** and **MRS. THOMPSON** turn and start to exit when **CHARLIE** enters from the other side of the stage, carrying a mailbag and a stack of mail.)*

CHARLIE. You guys headed home?

*(**MRS. THOMPSON** stops and turns.)*

MRS. THOMPSON. Charlie! What are you doing here?

CHARLIE. I realized I never gave you your mail when I stopped by earlier.

(He hands her the stack of envelopes.)

Here you go.

MRS. THOMPSON. Thank you. But how did you get here? The parking lots and roads are completely covered in snow.

CHARLIE. It's like I told you before – *(Raising his hand and reciting.)* Neither snow nor rain nor heat nor gloom of night stays these couriers from the swift completion of their appointed rounds.

PEGGY. And did you get your rounds completed in all this snow?

CHARLIE. I sure did! And now the day is done. Can I help you two get home?

>   *(**MRS. THOMPSON** and **PEGGY** turn to one another.)*

PEGGY. Well –

MRS. THOMPSON. Home?

PEGGY. It's up to you.

>   *(**MRS. THOMPSON** smiles at **CHARLIE**.)*

MRS. THOMPSON. Thanks for your kind offer, Charlie, but Peggy and I here have ourselves quite the evening planned.

PEGGY. We're going to have day-old meatloaf!

CHARLIE. *(Chuckles.)* Yum.

MRS. THOMPSON. So if it's all the same to you, I think we're going to be snowed in tonight.

CHARLIE. Sounds good.

>   *(He tips his cap.)*

See you both tomorrow.

MRS. THOMPSON. See you then!

>   *(**CHARLIE** exits. **MRS. THOMPSON** and **PEGGY** turn to exit.)*

PEGGY. You know, since we're staying the night, if we have a snow day tomorrow, it'll be easy to film another snow day announcement.

> (**MRS. THOMPSON** *stops and turns to the audience.*)

MRS. THOMPSON. *(Aghast.)* Another snow day?

(She smiles.)

Works for me!

> (**MRS. THOMPSON** *exits with* **PEGGY** *as lights fade to black.*)

End of Play

Scene 4: Snow Queen
(Alternate Version)

*(Outside. **ALEXIS** enters, deflated, carrying a garland of cut-paper snowflakes. She wears a fancy dress with a scarf and earmuffs. **NADIA**, **MADDIE**, **JEN**, and **EMMA** enter. One of them is carrying a bag, which they drop as they rush to **ALEXIS**.)*

NADIA. We came as soon as we heard!

ALEXIS. I can't believe it.

MADDIE. I know.

ALEXIS. What are the odds?

JEN. A million to one, I'd guess.

ALEXIS. The weatherman said it was supposed to be clear skies all week!

EMMA. Well, you never can trust a weatherman.

ALEXIS. But a snowstorm on the day of the Snowcoming Dance? *(Dramatically.)* It's too much to bear!

*(**ALEXIS** collapses in sobs. **NADIA** bends down to console her.)*

NADIA. Everything is going to be alright, Alexis. It's just a dance.

*(**ALEXIS** looks up, teary-eyed.)*

ALEXIS. Just a dance?

(She stands, aghast.)

JUST A DANCE?

*(She turns away from **NADIA**.)*

How can you say such a thing when you know how hard I've been working on this?

NADIA. I know. You're right. I'm sorry. I shouldn't have said that.

(**ALEXIS** *holds up snowflake garland.*)

ALEXIS. Look at these snowflakes.

(*She pushes them closer to* **NADIA**'s *face.*)

LOOK AT THEM!

MADDIE. We're looking, we're looking!

ALEXIS. Do you know how long it took me to cut these out? How many hours of painstaking work went into each and every snowflake to make them as distinct and unique as the members of our entire student body?

JEN. I don't know...a lot?

ALEXIS. Yes, Jen...a lot. Like, a lot, a lot. And do you know how many snowman sugar cookies I have sitting at home, each decorated with a sugar carrot nose and hat?

JEN. A dozen?

ALEXIS. Try twelve dozen.

EMMA. (*Smirking.*) So that's like...a dozen dozen?

ALEXIS. (*Annoyed.*) Really, Emma?

EMMA. Sorry. I was just trying to lighten the mood. My bad.

ALEXIS. And do you know how much time I spent handpicking each song on the Snowcoming playlist?

MADDIE. Actually, I do know that one, because I was right there with you when we picked the songs.

ALEXIS. Oh, that's right. That was a fun night.

MADDIE. It sure was.

(**ALEXIS** *lifts the hem of her dress.*)

ALEXIS. But do you know how long it took me to find this dress? A dress so flowy, so sparkly, so perfect that only a queen should wear it.

NADIA. *(Gently.)* A Snow Queen maybe?

ALEXIS. *(Sadly, not thinking.)* Yes. *(Quickly.)* I mean no! I mean...of course I didn't expect to be crowned Snow Queen...but you never know...and if I was, I just wanted to look the part...and... *(Sighs.)* And now it's all for nothing. School's closed for a snow day and the dance is cancelled.

MADDIE. They could reschedule it, you know.

ALEXIS. No, they can't. I already talked to Mrs. Thompson. Apparently the cafetorium is booked solid for the next month. Peggy checked the calendar three times.

JEN. So that's it then?

ALEXIS. Yep. That's it.

> (*She holds up one end of the garland and looks at it.*)

I guess I might as well throw these away.

> (*She starts to drop the snowflake garland.*)

EMMA. Wait!

> (**EMMA** *rushes over and grabs the garland before it falls.*)

ALEXIS. It doesn't matter anymore, Emma. Don't you see?

EMMA. We do see. We've seen it all along.

> (**EMMA** *takes a step forward.*)

Have you?

ALEXIS. What –

NADIA. We've seen how much you care, not only about this dance, but about everyone at this school.

MADDIE. How you wanted everything to be just right.

JEN. How you wanted everyone to feel special.

EMMA. You wanted everything to be perfect.

ALEXIS. I did.

NADIA. But don't you see? The most perfect thing isn't a paper snowflake or a sugar-cookie snowman.

MADDIE. It's not even this beautiful dress.

JEN. It's amazing friends like you, Alexis. You're the reason I joined the dance committee.

MADDIE. Me too. You're the reason I stayed up late picking songs.

EMMA. You're the reason we rushed over here the second we heard that the dance was cancelled.

*(***NADIA*** picks up the bag and takes out a tiara.)*

NADIA. You're our Snow Queen, Alexis. And you don't need a dance to earn this crown.

*(She puts the tiara on ***ALEXIS****'s head.)*

ALEXIS. I...I don't know what to say.

MADDIE. I say...we have a dance party, right here and right now!

ALEXIS. Out here in the snow? Are you crazy?

JEN. Why not?

ALEXIS. Only because it's freezing out here!

(She smiles.)

ALEXIS. I have a better idea. Let's go inside where it's warmer. We can turn on the playlist and dig into those snowman cookies.

EMMA. Sounds good to me!

NADIA. Me too!

MADDIE. Lead the way, Your Majesty.

(**ALEXIS** *exits royally as others follow and lights fade to black.*)

www.ingramcontent.com/pod-product-compliance
Lightning Source LLC
Chambersburg PA
CBHW051007060726

47593CB00017B/1221